MANAGING INTERNATIONAL MARKETS
A Survey of Training Practices and Emerging Trends

A. KAPOOR

Graduate School of Business Administration,

New York University

ROBERT J. McKAY

Director, Marketing Planning,

Pan American World Airways

THE DARWIN PRESS

Princeton, New Jersey

Library of Congress Catalog Card Number: 79-161052

To Catherine and Patricia

ISBN 0-87850-002-2 (cloth)
ISBN 0-87850-003-0 (paper)

Printed in the United States of America

CONTENTS

LIST OF FIGURES AND TABLES

PREFATORY NOTE AND ACKNOWLEDGEMENTS

The large American companies which are the subject of this study have been the leaders in the dramatic growth of international business during the past two decades. The growth will continue in the 1970s and beyond, and as in the 1950s and 1960s, the coming decades will present new challenges to business. Some of the challenges will be new (greater integration of worldwide operations), some will be old (language ability, trade restrictions), and some will be familiar but expressed in a new context (economic and political nationalism). A company's ability to cope with these challenges will depend upon the quality of its personnel and their ability to anticipate, plan for, and benefit from these challenges.

This volume deals with training for managing international markets. It should prove useful for both the corporate executive and the student of international business. Executives responsible for international marketing operations will find the book directly relevant to their work by answering such questions as what are the general characteristics of international marketing and what is the nature of the training program and of the international marketing personnel.

Non-marketing executives will also find the book useful. Environmental factors, the stress on the integration of worldwide operations, the emphasis on domestic on-the-job training for international assignments—these and other issues relevant to executives responsible for general management and international accounting, financing, and production are dealt with extensively.

An ever increasing number of schools of business administration in the United States and overseas are offering courses in international business, and international marketing is the subject most frequently taught. This study provides the student of international marketing with the concepts, methods, and techniques required for training executives for the management of international markets. In addition, courses on international management will also find the book useful through its coverage of the major issues of international business—functional integration, environmental factors, and relevance of domestic experience.

The book offers information on the existing state of the field and the likely pattern of future evolution in training for the management of international markets. However, the observations are not the final word on the subject; additional research is required on several critical issues only highlighted in these pages.

An important characteristic facilitating additional research is the form in which the information on training for the management of international markets has been presented. The data in the tables and in the appendixes will permit other researchers to explore the relationship between one or more variables. For example, a corporate executive can gain general ideas on training methods which are particularly relevant for a company of a particular size, overseas sales, and primary product. Or, one can explore whether there is a relationship between a company's overseas sales and the existing or anticipated shortage of qualified international marketing personnel.

A significant body of additional information is available from the raw data which formed the basis for the tables in this study. The authors are willing to share the data with other interested researchers.

We wish to extend our thanks to Mr. Robert J. Small for his careful rechecking of the tabulation of the response and his general assistance in the development of the book.

We appreciated the comments of Dr. J. Maldutis and Mr. J. Lorenzo during the early phases of this study.

We also wish to express our appreciation to Miss Gail Rubinsky and Miss Sheila Fitzpatrick for their typing of the various drafts of the manuscript and to Miss Lynette Cunningham for her patience in editing the manuscript through its various stages of completion.

Of course, without the understanding shown by our wives this book would not have been possible.

A. Kapoor
Robert J. McKay

New York City

INTRODUCTION

International business, unlike domestic, involves operations in social-cultural-economic-political environments which vary by country.[1] The specific techniques of a function (quantitative analysis for marketing management) can be extended across national boundaries. However, their effectiveness is determined by the extent to which such techniques do not conflict with environmental factors. For example, market research techniques requiring electronic data processing in many developing countries are impractical for the simple reason that such countries lack the necessary physical facilities and trained personnel.

There are four major differences between domestic and international business. First, *the international environmental context is relatively unknown,* because most American companies have only recently become aware of overseas markets. Again, some environments are better known by some companies; for example, Europe and Latin America are better known to American companies because they are culturally similar and they account for a large percentage of American private foreign investment. However, Asia, Africa, and the Middle East are less known.[2]

Second, *the environmental context of foreign countries is different from that of the United States.* However, ethnocentrism (the tendency to evaluate a foreign context with reference to one's own) is a major characteristic of the American and the foreign businessman alike.[3]

Third, the physical distances separating executives in international business cause serious *problems of communication.* Problems of language, semantic differences, inadequate communication facilities, and time differences are significantly different from those encountered by a business operating in a single country.

Fourth, most *American companies are largely oriented towards the domestic market.* Therefore, the most senior levels of management (chief operating officers, members of the board) and other top management levels (division chiefs) have a far greater understanding of and interest in domestic than in international operations.[4] Chorafas states that, according to the executives he interviewed, international operations accounting for less than

1

30% of the total corporate income are relegated to an inferior status and are staffed by lower caliber executives than in the case of domestic operations.[5] For these reasons, the executives engaged in international operations are faced with the major task of educating their management colleagues about the nature and significance of international operations.

Cumulative private foreign investment by American companies has reached the staggering figure of almost $140 billion in market value.[6] While the giant and large companies are the major investors, medium and small companies are participating in the growing volume of international investments and will continue to do so.

The unique characteristics of international business together with a rapid growth have created problems for companies in the areas of personnel and overall organization structure. Executives with experience in international business are in short supply, as noted by Duerr and Greene[7] and Gonzales and Negandhi[8]; and Lovell observes that corporations have made a great effort to alter the nature of the international assignment so that it fits the capabilities of the selected executive.[9]

While Gonzales and Negandhi stress cultural empathy as a necessary qualification for international business executives, they point out that the lack of such empathy is the reason why the effective staffing of international positions is more difficult than that of the domestic.[10] Ivancevich notes that the executives (foreign operations manager, overseas manager) responding to his survey stated that an interest in foreign cultures was not an important factor in their being chosen for an assignment overseas. Yet, the same executives also stated that the inability of their predecessors to adapt to the different physical/cultural environments overseas was the primary reason for their lack of effectiveness[11] —an observation which is supported by Lovell.[12]

Chorafas notes that cultural empathy (understanding and adapting to foreign environments) is seldom stressed in the training of international business executives. Rather, these executives are trained in programs which are oriented almost exclusively towards a domestic environment. Chorafas adds that this is largely due to the lesser importance attached to international business by senior management.[13]

Objectives

The observations resulting from the studies on international business training are relevant in training for international marketing management. However, a systematic study of the nature and content of training for international marketing offered by the large American corporation has not been undertaken. Admittedly, managing international markets imposes upon the manager a number of responsibilities (a greater awareness of the environment) not shared to the same extent in accounting, finance, and production.

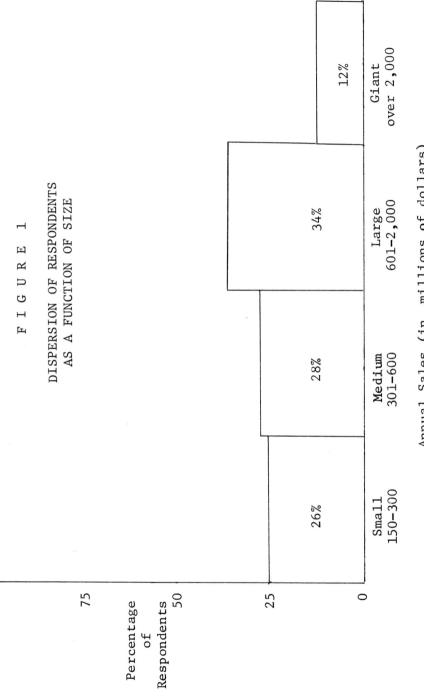

F I G U R E   1

DISPERSION OF RESPONDENTS
AS A FUNCTION OF SIZE

Percentage of Respondents

Annual Sales (in millions of dollars)

Small 150–300: 26%
Medium 301–600: 28%
Large 601–2,000: 34%
Giant over 2,000: 12%

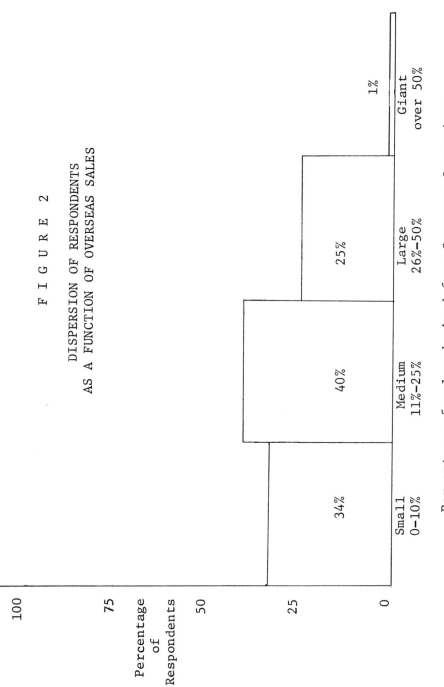

F I G U R E 2

DISPERSION OF RESPONDENTS
AS A FUNCTION OF OVERSEAS SALES

Percentage of sales derived from Overseas Operations

This study summarizes the present state of training for international marketing management and attempts to answer the following questions.

1. **Domestic and International:** What are the major international marketing *problem area?* What are the major *differences* between domestic and international marketing?

2. **International marketing training program:**
   Who is *selected*?
   At *what organization level* is the training program conducted, *by whom,* and using *what methods*?
   What are the *primary objectives*?
   What *changes* are anticipated and *why*?
   What features of *foreign environment training* are included and *in what ways and why* will they change?

3. **International marketing personnel:**
   Are international and domestic marketing skills *transferable*?
   What are the major *difficulties* faced?
   What characteristics favor *success*?
   What is the *existing and anticipated* supply?

4. **Size and commitment:** What is the effect of *company size, extent of overseas sales,* and *nature of products* on the international marketing management training program?

Methodology

A sample of 384 firms having verifiable overseas operations was extracted from the *Fortune* list of the top 500 firms in the United States. These companies were surveyed in the spring of 1970 by mail questionnaires. The response rate was a gratifying 35.4%—i.e., 136 returns out of 384. Of this amount 30%, or 116 returns, were completed in full; seventeen companies declined to answer any part of the questionnaire because of company policy, while three returned questionnaires which could not be used.

Figure 1 presents the dispersion of respondents in terms of annual sales using the classification of small, medium, large, and giant. The distribution of the respondents as a function of size (annual sales in millions of dollars) is as follows: small ($150-300)—26%; medium ($301-600)—28%; large ($601-2,000)—34%; giant (over $2,000)—12%.

Figure 2 presents the dispersion of respondents in terms of the percentage of sales derived from overseas operations. Only in one case did international sales account for more than 50% of total sales. For slightly over 25% of the respondents, international sales comprised between 26-50% of total sales. The remaining respondents were distributed as follows— 40%: 11-25% sales; and 34%: 0-10% sales.

The primary market divided approximately 60/40 between industry and consumers, with less than 15% of the respondents indicating they dealt with various other groups, e.g., physicians and hospitals, the U. S. military abroad. Only 3.5% of the responses indicated host governments as the primary customer.

1
PROFILE OF RESPONDING COMPANIES

GENERAL CHARACTERISTICS

Major International Marketing Problems

Nearly one-quarter of the responses indicate that the integration of international marketing into a worldwide corporate effort is a major problem. Approximately 16% of the respondents listed lack of marketing data in international marketing as the major problem, while unsuitable distribution channels was a problem listed by 12% of the respondents. Others gave trade barriers (10%), unfair competition (9%), local legal and political complications (8%), and scarcity of personnel (8%) as significant problems.

TABLE 1

MAJOR INTERNATIONAL MARKETING PROBLEMS

	No.	%
Integration of International Marketing into Worldwide Corporate Effort	28	24
Lack of Marketing Data	18	16
Unsuitable Distribution Channels	14	12
Trade Barriers	12	10
Unfair Competition	10	9
Local Legal and Political Complications	9	8
Scarcity of Personnel	9	8
Increasing Nationalism	6	4
Product Adaptation to Local Use	5	4
Other/Multiple Unranked	3	3
No Response	2	2
TOTAL	116	100

(The problem of staffing overseas marketing positions is analyzed below, and a detailed breakdown of responses is presented in Tables 15 and 16.)

7

Problems in adapting products to local use and increasing nationalism were cited by 4%. Apparently nationalism is not seen as an international marketing problem.

Differences Between Domestic and International Marketing

Table 2 shows that 13% of the respondents do not see any significant difference between domestic and international marketing. The greatest single difference noted, 24%, was of greater government (largely foreign) regulation. The response to integration of international marketing both at the corporate and division level was next in importance with 15%. However, the importance of integration is also included in the responses of 12% each on the need for more feedback and control in international marketing as well as the need for greater awareness of international marketing problems by top management. A greater need for data and the existence of a lesser consumer orientation in international marketing were indicated by 9% and 3%, respectively.

TABLE 2

DOMESTIC AND INTERNATIONAL MARKETING DIFFERENCES

	No.	%
Greater International Government Regulation	28	24
No Significant Difference	15	13
Need for More Feedback/Control in International Marketing	14	12
Less Awareness of International Problems by Top Management	14	12
Need for More Data in International Marketing	10	9
Greater Need to Integrate International Marketing at Division Level	10	9
at Corporate Level	7	6
Greater Emphasis on Consumer Orientation in Domestic Marketing	4	3
Other/Multiple Unranked	12	10
No Response	2	2
TOTAL	116	100

INTERNATIONAL MARKETING TRAINING PROGRAM

Selection Criteria

Forty percent of the respondents listed a proven domestic marketing ability as the primary prerequisite for candidates for overseas marketing positions. However, 25% cited foreign national status, and only 16% cited interest in the field of international marketing as a key prerequisite. Another 10%

TABLE 3

PERSONNEL SELECTION CRITERIA

	No.	%
Proven Domestic Marketing Ability	46	40
Foreign National Status	29	25
Those Expressing Interest	18	16
Prior Formal Training	12	10
Preparation for Eventual Greater Domestic Responsibility	6	5
Foreign Language Ability	2	2
No Response	3	2
TOTAL	116	100

listed prior formal training—such as a degree in international business—as being essential. Preparation for eventual greater domestic responsibility and foreign language ability accounted for 5% and 2%, respectively.

The Program Method

The primary domestic orientation revealed in Table 3 is also reflected in Table 4. Approximately 43% of the respondents indicated on-the-job training in the United States as the preferred method of training. This figure also implies that marketing skills are transferable from a domestic to a foreign environment (also borne out by Table 12) and that marketing mechanics which are universal take precedence over training in a foreign environment (also borne out by Table 7). Taken together with the 32% reporting international on-the-job training, responding companies seem to favor the on-the-job method to alternative training methods 3 to 1. The regular company training program is most popular among these alternative methods, accounting for 10% of total responses.

TABLE 4

METHOD OF CONDUCTING PROGRAM

	No.	%
Domestic On-the-Job Training	50	43
International On-the-Job Training	37	32
Formal Company Program	11	10
Formal Outside Program	1	1
Seminar Type Courses	1	1
Other/Multiple Unranked	12	10
No Response	4	3
TOTAL	116	100

Who Conducts the Program

Table 5 shows that slightly over one-third of the respondents place the responsibility of international marketing training on the international division. Another 22% place the responsibility with the international marketing group. Thus, 56% of the respondents conduct their training programs through the international division of the total organization. In fact, this figure is likely to be higher because a percentage of the response under

TABLE 5

WHO CONDUCTS THE PROGRAM

	No.	%
International Division	39	34
International Marketing Group	26	22
Marketing Department	17	15
Functional Supervisor	16	14
Professional Association	1	1
Other/Multiple Unranked	9	8
No Response	8	6
TOTAL	116	100

"Marketing Department" (15%) and "Functional Supervisor" (14%) would be organizationally related to the international division of a company.

Noticeable is the absence in the training programs of outside courses and seminars, such as those offered by professional associations, consulting firms, and colleges and universities.

Level

Thirty-one percent of the respondents answered that the training program is offered at the international division level.

TABLE 6

LEVELS AT WHICH PROGRAM IS OFFERED

	No.	%
International Division	35	31
All Levels	20	17
Where needed or no Particular Level	20	17
No Internal Program Offered	14	12
Regional	8	7
Individual Country	7	6
Corporate	4	3
No Response	8	7
TOTAL	116	100

In Table 6 it is again evident that a few firms—only 12%—do not have an internally administered program. However, nearly half of the responses indicate that firms offer programs at several levels; for example, all levels —corporate, international, regional, country—(17%); where needed or at no particular level (17%); regional (7%); and individual country level (6%). Only 3% of the respondents report programs on the corporate level.

Program Objectives

For 25% of the respondents, the primary objective of the training program is to offer a survey of international marketing; specifics of government account for another 9% of the total; and specific product and selling knowledge also account for 9%. An emphasis on worldwide marketing orientation, which accounts for 23% of the responses, indicates companies have assigned high priority to meeting the challenge of the major international marketing problem, i.e., integration of international marketing into a worldwide corporate effort, reported in Table 1. However, an important

TABLE 7

PRIMARY OBJECTIVES OF PROGRAM

	No.	%
Overall Survey of International Marketing	30	25
Stress Importance of Integration of International Marketing into Unified Corporate Effort	27	23
Stress Concrete Characteristics such as Greater Government Regulation	10	9
Impart Specific Product and Selling Knowledge	10	9
Cultural Sensitization	7	7
Demonstrate Abstract Differences Such as Lesser Consumer Orientation Abroad	4	3
Other/Multiple Unranked	10	9
No Response	18	15
TOTAL	116	100

question is whether the present program methods (Table 4) and responsibility levels (Tables 5 and 6) are likely to be adequate to achieve the objective of greater integration. Only 7% of the responses stressed the importance of cultural sensitization.

Expected Changes

Table 8 shows how respondents view their training programs in five years. Thus, 34% of the respondents stress integration of international marketing into a worldwide corporate effort. Another 26% project greater stress on sales and distribution techniques, a point emphasized in Table 10. Another 13% of the respondents stress product adaptability, while 10% mention structural changes such as introduction of formal programs.

It should be noted that a mere 6% of the respondents favored increased stress on achieving greater awareness of socio-political aspects of foreign environments (3%) and of local language and customs (3%). Table 8 suggests that international marketing techniques are likely to become far more important in the training program than environmental factors. Tables 10 and 12 elaborate further on these points.

TABLE 8

EXPECTED CHANGES IN PROGRAM

	No.	*%*
Greater Stress on Integrating International Marketing into Worldwide Corporate Effort	39	34
Greater Stress on Sales and Distribution Techniques	29	26
Greater Stress on Product Adaptability	15	13
Structural Changes Such as Introduction of Formal Training Programs	12	10
Greater Stress on Socio-Political Aspects Such as Nationalism	4	3
Greater Stress on Local Characteristics Such as Language and Customs	4	3
No Response	13	11
TOTAL	116	100

Reasons for Change

By far the major reason for change (30%) in the training program would be the evolution of an overall international market (i.e., greater uniformity of

TABLE 9

REASONS FOR CHANGE

	No.	*%*
Development of Worldwide Marketing Effort	34	30
More Sophisticated Products Introduced into Less Developed Countries	19	16
More Effective, Vigorous Local Competition	19	16
Greater Consumer Orientation Abroad	15	12
Greater Cooperation With Local Interests	9	8
Other/Multiple Unranked	7	7
No Response	13	11
TOTAL	116	100

markets) rather than the existing pattern of several individual foreign markets. Of course, such an evolution will place greater stress on a world-wide marketing effort. Greater efficiency in the areas of sales and distribution techniques in foreign markets will be due to more effective and vigorous local competition (16%) coupled with increasing consumer orientation abroad (12%). Growth of competition in foreign markets will require greater product adaptation, a characteristic which is likely to be reflected in the process of introducing more sophisticated products into less developed countries (16%). These developments are likely to require greater cooperation with local partners and middlemen (8%).

Foreign Environment Training

A large majority of the respondents (59%) emphasize teaching marketing techniques peculiar to overseas marketing in the training program. Another 16% emphasize the ability to speak a foreign language and a knowledge of local business traits, while 5% stress an understanding of the broader social-cultural aspects of a foreign environment.

TABLE 10

FOREIGN ENVIRONMENT TRAINING IN PROGRAM

	No.	%
Marketing Techniques Peculiar to Overseas Operations	69	59
Specifics Such as Language	18	16
Concepts Such as Socio-Cultural Differences	6	5
Other/Multiple Unranked	9	8
No Response	14	12
TOTAL	116	100

Table 11 shows that 23% of the respondents do not foresee changes in the components of the training program. However, other respondents expect them and 19% of the respondents believe that product sophistication will require greater product knowledge. A theme reflected in Tables 8 and 9 is repeated in Table 11, where, 16% mention the development of a trend toward a world customer as opposed to a highly unique individual country market. Again, foreign environment training will stress the nature of local competition, thus resulting in a better identification of consumers (10%) and in a need for greater empathy with a foreign market/culture because of greater consumer orientation (10%).

TABLE 11

EXPECTED CHANGES IN FOREIGN ENVIRONMENT TRAINING

	No.	%
No Change	26	23
Product Sophistication Will Require Greater Product Knowledge	21	19
Trend Toward World Customer Will Develop	19	16
Consumer Orientation Will Require More Empathy	12	10
More Local Competition Will Require Better Consumer Identification	12	10
Other/Multiple Unranked	6	5
No Response	20	17
TOTAL	116	100

INTERNATIONAL MARKETING PERSONNEL

Transferability of Marketing Skills

Slightly over a third of the respondents (35%) indicated that marketing skills are transferable from one country to another (Table 12). However, there is a marked difference in the direction of the transfer; thus, 22% of

TABLE 12

TRANSFERABILITY OF MARKETING SKILLS

	No.	%
Mutually Transferable	40	35
Depends on Individual	39	34
Domestic Transferable to International	26	22
International Transferable to Domestic	4	3
Neither Transferable	3	3
Other/Multiple Unranked	4	3
TOTAL	116	100

the respondents believe that domestic marketing skills can be transferred to international operations. (In Table 3 we saw that proven domestic marketing ability is the main criterion in selecting personnel for overseas operations; these companies are likely to stress the transferability of domestic marketing skills to the international sphere.) One-third (34%) of the respondents stated that transferability depends on the individual, but only 3% of the respondents believe that international marketing skills can be extended to the domestic (U.S.) context.

Problems

Slightly over one-third (34%) of the respondents regarded adapting to a different cultural environment as the main difficulty faced by international marketing personnel (Table 13). More specifically, most personnel assigned

TABLE 13

MAIN DIFFICULTY FACED BY INTERNATIONAL MARKETING PERSONNEL

	No.	%
Adapting to Different Cultural Concepts	39	34
Being out of Corporate Mainstream	37	32
Different Standard of Living	20	17
Language Barrier	10	9
Other/Multiple Unranked	5	4
No Response	5	4
TOTAL	116	100

overseas find it difficult to accept the lower (relative to the U. S.) standards of living (e.g., inadequate educational system, lack of items regarded as necessities in the U. S.), a point mentioned by 17% of the respondents. For another 9%, the inability to speak a foreign language (e.g., an American trying to do business in Japan) is an important handicap experienced by international marketing personnel.

Another difficulty which is not limited to international marketing personnel but applies to all positions involving international assignments is that of being out of the corporate mainstream (32%). This anxiety is due to two main reasons. First, for most companies the domestic (United States) market is by far the largest contributor to corporate sales and profits. Therefore, the relative power of those with domestic market responsibilities over important corporate policies and programs is far greater than that of the executive responsible for international operations. Second, personnel

assigned overseas fear that they may be forgotten by managers at headquarters in the U. S. when decisions are being made on matters of promotion or new assignments. Also, marketing personnel are likely to be
posted overseas for a longer time than personnel in accounting or finance
because the marketing function necessitates developing a more thorough
understanding of a foreign environment.

Reasons for Success

Table 14 indicates that almost one-fourth of the respondents agree that a
strong sense of empathy with a foreign environment is a prerequisite for

TABLE 14

CHARACTERISTICS FAVORING SUCCESS
IN INTERNATIONAL MARKETING POSITIONS

	No.	*%*
Strong Empathy with Foreign Environment	28	24
Domestic Marketing Experience	26	22
Being National of Country of Assignment	18	16
Desire to Work Overseas	14	12
Corporate International Marketing Training	7	7
Foreign Language Ability	4	3
College or University Training	4	3
Other/Multiple Unranked	13	11
No Response	2	2
TOTAL	116	100

success overseas. This observation is consistent with the heavy reliance on
foreign nationals as indicated in the staffing criteria of Table 3 and again in
Table 14. However, a paradox emerges insofar as the main difficulty
experienced by American personnel overseas (Table 13) is primarily one of
cultural adjustment; besides, neither an expressed interest in international
marketing nor a cultural sensitivity appear to be important prerequisites for
overseas candidacy (Table 3). Even more paradoxical is the fact that a
strong empathy with the foreign environment is a characteristic for success
of all overseas personnel, and, yet, its inculcation is a low-priority objective
of the training program (Table 7). Consequently, proven domestic (U. S.)
marketing ability plus additional on-the-job training in the U. S. before the
assignment overseas appear perfectly consonant with the 22% reporting that
a domestic marketing experience contributes to success overseas.

Shortage of Personnel

The respondents frequently complained of an acute shortage of international marketing personnel in both the short and the long runs—63% and 59% respectively as shown in Table 15. Only a minority claimed that a surplus of trained personnel exists today and will exist five years from now—12% and 9% respectively. Another slightly more significant minority cited no shortage today or in the future—22% and 29% respectively.

TABLE 15

AVAILABILITY OF QUALIFIED INTERNATIONAL MARKETING PERSONNEL

	Today		In Five Years	
	No.	%	No.	%
Supply Less than Demand	73	63	68	59
Supply Greater than Demand	14	12	10	9
Supply Equal To Demand	25	22	34	29
No Response	4	3	4	3
TOTAL	116	100	116	100

Reasons for Shortage of Personnel

Generally, shortages of international marketing personnel are attributed to shortages of qualified marketing personnel—34% and 24% in the short and

TABLE 16

REASONS FOR SHORTAGE OF INTERNATIONAL MARKETING PERSONNEL

	Today		In Five Years	
	No.	%	No.	%
General Shortage of Marketing Personnel	39	34	28	24
No Shortage	22	19	21	18
Unwillingness to Live Abroad	20	16	22	19
Abstract Nature of International Marketing	18	17	15	13
Lack of College Level Training Programs	5	4	1	1
No Response	12	10	29	25
TOTAL	116	100	116	100

long runs respectively. Other respondents were more specific, as Table 16 indicates, many blaming the abstract nature of international marketing problems—largely composed of social-cultural factors—and the lack of college level training programs for it. A significant minority claimed an unwillingness to live abroad as a factor affecting personnel availability today (16%) and over the next five years (19%).

2

TRAINING FOR INTERNATIONAL MARKETING:

SELECTED VARIABLES*

This chapter explores the effect of firm size, extent of international sales, and product line on the training program. To make it easier and to avoid an overabundance of detail, the firm size and overseas sales of the responding companies have been categorized as small, medium, large, and giant, yielding a 4 x 4 matrix, as in Table 17.

Table 17 shows that there is a sizeable distribution of small, medium, and large firms with up to 50% of total sales revenues realized from foreign operations. The distribution is scanty for giant firms.

TABLE 17

DISTRIBUTION OF RESPONDENTS: SIZE AND INTERNATIONAL SALES**

International Sales as Percent of Total Sales		Size of Firms			
	%	Small	Medium	Large	Giant
Small	0-10	10	16	12	2
Medium	11-25	13	11	16	6
Large	26-50	7	6	11	5
World	51 +	0	0	0	1
		30	33	39	14

*A detailed tabulation of responses relating to specific questions is offered in Appendixes C through F.

**International or overseas sales refers to some percentage of total company sales in markets outside of the domestic (United States) market.

SIZE OF FIRM AND EXTENT OF OVERSEAS SALES*

Major International Marketing Problems

Companies, regardless of size and extent of overseas sales, regard integration of international marketing into the overall marketing effort as the major problem at present (Table C-1). Additionally, large companies, especially those with medium overseas sales, regard the lack of marketing data as a major problem, an observation also shared by the small- and medium-size companies. Again, large companies regard the lack of suitable distribution channels overseas as an important international marketing problem, a view shared by the small and medium-size companies. And medium-size companies with small and medium levels of overseas sales stress the shortage of qualified personnel.

Differences Between Domestic and International Marketing

Table C-2 shows that companies, regardless of size and overseas sales, consider more government regulations as the major difference between domestic and international marketing. And the need for greater feedback of information and control in international marketing is shared by companies in all categories, but with medium-size companies stressing this point. Companies of all sizes stress top management's lesser awareness of international marketing (and business in general) problems. Again, the need for integration of international marketing at the corporate and division level is stressed by all companies. However, large companies, especially those with medium overseas sales, emphasize the need for more data in international marketing.

INTERNATIONAL MARKETING TRAINING PROGRAM

Criteria for Personnel Selection

Regardless of size of overseas sales, companies place the greatest weight on proven domestic marketing ability in the selection of personnel for interna-

---

*A detailed tabulation of responses relating to specific questions on international sales *and* size of firm is offered in Tables C-1 through C-18. Appendixes D and E contain a tabulation of the response as it relates *specifically* to firm size (Appendix D) and to international sales (Appendix E). The analysis presented in this section contains the essential characteristics revealed in Appendixes C and F.

tional marketing assignments (Table C-3). Companies of all sizes with medium overseas sales are the ones which stress this characteristic in particular. Also, companies of all sizes and overseas sales stress "foreign national status" (being a national of the country). Medium- and small-size firms, especially with small and medium overseas sales, stress an interest in international marketing by the applicant as the main selection criterion. Table C-3 shows that formal training (such as a university degree in international marketing or international business) is often a criterion for selection.

It should be noted in Table C-3 that none of the small companies, regardless of overseas sales, consider international marketing assignments as an important step in training executives for greater responsibilities at the corporate (domestic) level. A handful of medium-size firms with small overseas sales and some large firms with small and large overseas sales seem to view international marketing assignments as an important step in overall career development. However, this is a far less important criterion than others.

The Program

Table C-4 shows that all companies consider domestic (in the United States) on-the-job training as the major method of training international marketing managers. To a lesser extent, all types of companies also use international on-the-job training. Regardless of company size and overseas sales, the use of outside programs (by universities, professional organizations) is almost completely absent.

Who Conducts the Program

Many companies in all categories of size and international sales charge the international division with the responsibility for conducting the training program (Table C-5). This approach is stressed by the small- and medium-size companies with small and medium overseas sales, and also by large companies in all categories of overseas sales. The marketing department is mentioned by all companies, but medium-size companies in all overseas sales categories place particular emphasis on it. Small companies with small overseas sales and large companies with large overseas sales do not appear to conduct the training program through their marketing departments.

The international marketing group (which might be part of the international division or a separate corporate-wide functional group, depending on the organization structure of a company) is used by all companies with the exception of small companies with large overseas sales. Large companies, particularly those with small overseas sales, usually use the international marketing group to conduct the training program.

Level

Many companies in all size and overseas sales categories offer training programs at the division level (Table C-6). Medium and large firms with small and medium overseas sales strongly favor the division level. Also, many companies—especially the small and large companies with medium overseas sales—do not offer training at any one particular level but on a where-needed basis. A number of companies in all categories of size do not have any training programs of their own. Again, companies in all size categories offer training at all levels—corporate, division, regional, and country. This approach seems to be preferred by small-size companies with large overseas sales, medium-size companies with small overseas sales, and large companies with large overseas sales.

Program Objectives

Table C-7 shows that a wide spectrum of companies regard a general survey of international marketing as the primary objective of the training program. However, small-size firms with medium overseas sales, medium-size firms with small and medium overseas sales, and large firms in all overseas sales categories emphasize this objective.

Again, all categories of companies stress educating executives on the integration of international marketing at the corporate level. This point is mentioned in particular by the medium-size firms with small overseas sales and by large companies with medium overseas sales.

All companies seek to impart a knowledge of the specific characteristics of international marketing (e.g., government regulations) and a knowledge of specific products and the manner of selling them in the international markets.

Expected Changes

Table C-8 shows that companies expect changes in the present training programs. All companies expect very soon to be educating executives on the integration of international marketing at the corporate level. However, this point is stressed by small-size firms with small overseas sales, medium-size firms with small and medium overseas sales, and all large-size firms but particularly in the medium overseas sales category.

Again, all companies expect to place greater emphasis on training in sales and distribution techniques in international marketing. This point is noted in particular by small firms with small and medium overseas sales and by medium-size firms with small and medium overseas sales.

Greater training in product adaptation will figure more prominently in the training programs of almost all companies. But large companies with small overseas sales are particularly aware of this point.

More formal training programs (based on a careful review of content, objectives, methods, etc.) are envisioned by many companies, especially those of medium and large size.

Reasons for Change

A major reason for anticipated changes in the training program for all companies is the development of an overall, world market concept, e.g., product and marketing methods are developed for potential worldwide use or at least regional (Western Europe) use (Table C-9). This point is stressed by medium-size firms with small and medium overseas sales and by large-size companies with medium and large overseas sales.

As we saw earlier, almost all companies anticipate increasing competition and envision greater consumer orientation in foreign markets—characteristics making such markets more similar to the U.S. market. Many companies in almost all categories of size and overseas sales expect changes in the training program because of the introduction of more sophisticated products into less developed countries. Small-size firms with medium overseas sales emphasize this point.

Foreign Environment Training

Table C-10 shows that the vast majority of companies consider a knowledge of international marketing techniques as the major aspect of foreign environment training. Conversely, emphasis on cultural differences in training are noted by only a handful of firms in the medium- and large-size categories. Large-size companies with large overseas sales appear to be the only ones attaching particular importance to cultural differences.

A representative distribution of companies recognize the need for training in specific aspects of the foreign environment, such as language and government regulations.

Expected Changes in Foreign Environment Training

As noted in Table C-11, several companies in almost all sizes and overseas sales categories do not anticipate changes in their international marketing training programs. However, a sizeable number of companies anticipate changes in this area.

Almost all companies, but notably large companies with medium and large overseas sales, expect the development of a trend toward the concept of a world customer. Again, several companies expect greater emphasis on knowledge of products by marketing personnel due to increasing (technical) sophistication of products. Medium- and large-size firms with small overseas sales place particular emphasis on this point.

Greater consumer empathy and consumer identification (because of local competition) are expected in foreign environment training by several companies in almost all categories. However, large-size companies appear to emphasize this characteristic in particular.

INTERNATIONAL MARKETING PERSONNEL

Transferability of Marketing Skills

Transferability of marketing skills depends on the individual executive (Table C-12). This point appears to be emphasized by medium- and large-size firms with small overseas sales.

A number of companies of different size and overseas sales categories are of the opinion that most domestic marketing skills can be transferred to international marketing. Large- and giant-size firms with medium overseas sales levels emphasize this point. Only a handful of firms, but none in the small-size category, believe that international marketing skills can be transferred to the domestic (U. S.) market.

However, a sizeable number of companies in nearly all categories—but particularly small-size firms with medium overseas sales and large-size firms with medium and large overseas sales—believe that domestic and international marketing skills are mutually transferable.

Problems

Table C-13 shows that companies in almost all categories consider being out of the corporate mainstream (e.g., away from corporate decision-making centers) a major problem faced by international marketing personnel. This point is stressed in particular by medium-size firms with small overseas sales and by large companies in all categories, especially those with medium overseas sales.

Companies in all categories of size and overseas sales—especially medium-size companies with medium overseas sales and large companies with small and medium overseas sales—are of the opinion that U. S. personnel have problems in adapting to foreign cultures.

Companies in almost all categories regard the standards of living overseas and, to a somewhat lesser extent, the difficulty of communication resulting from language differences as important problems for international marketing personnel.

Reasons for Success

For many companies in all categories—especially small-size firms with medium overseas sales and large firms with medium overseas sales—a domestic (U. S.) marketing experience is important for success in international marketing (Table C-14).

Again, for all types of companies, a strong sense of empathy with the foreign milieu is a key determinant of success of international marketing personnel. Medium-size companies with small overseas sales and large companies with medium overseas sales emphasize this point. Related to the point of empathy is the use of nationals in foreign countries, e.g., a Frenchman in France, a Mexican in Mexico, and so on. Several companies in many categories consider this practice important in the success of marketing personnel.

Companies in many categories of size and overseas sales consider the individual's desire to work overseas as important for his success in international marketing assignments. Medium-size firms with small overseas sales stress this point.

Shortage of Personnel

Table C-15 shows that for a majority of companies in all categories, the supply of qualified marketing personnel today is less than the demand. This point is emphasized by small-, medium-, and large-size firms with medium overseas sales.

A smaller number of companies in all categories of size and overseas sales believe that the supply of qualified personnel today is equal to the demand. An even smaller number of companies—especially medium-size companies with small overseas sales—feel that the supply today is greater than the demand.

Insofar as the supply of qualified personnel in the next five years is concerned (Table C-16), companies in all but one category are of the view that the supply will be less than the demand. This point is emphasized by small-size firms with medium overseas sales, medium-size firms with small and medium overseas sales, and large-size firms in all overseas sales categories, especially the medium and large ones.

A smaller number of companies—especially large firms with medium overseas sales—representing all categories feel that supply will equal demand in five years. An even smaller number of companies representing many categories are of the view that in five years the supply in fact will be greater than the demand.

Reasons for Shortage of Personnel

Table C-17 shows that a major reason for the current shortage of qualified personnel is the unwillingness of individuals to live abroad. Small-size firms with medium overseas sales stress this point.

As noted earlier, many companies in most categories believe that the current shortage is due to the abstract nature of international marketing and the difficulty of understanding and accepting social-cultural values different from one's own.

With regard to an anticipated future shortage of qualified personnel (C-18), companies in almost all categories of size and overseas sales believe it will result from an unwillingness to live abroad and from the abstract nature of international marketing.

FIRM'S PRIMARY CUSTOMER*

This section deals with the relationship between the training program and the firm's primary customers.

General Characteristics

Both industry- and consumer-oriented firms consider integrating international marketing operations at the corporate level as a major problem (Table F-1). However, the "Industry" group places a significantly greater weight on integration than the "Consumer" group; it also places a greater weight on the lack of marketing data. But both groups place about the same weight on the lack of suitable distribution channels.

---

*A detailed tabulation of the response by question relating to the firm's primary customer is offered in Tables F-1 through F-18. The two major categories of response are "Industry" and "Consumer" reflecting the broad categories of industrial and consumer goods. The response under the category of "Government" was limited. Also, a number of respondents chose the category of "Other."

Table F-2 refers to differences with respect to domestic and international marketing. Respondents from the Industry group believe that there are more government regulations and foresee the need for more data in the international sphere.

International Marketing Training Program

Both Industry and Consumer groups consider a proven domestic marketing ability as the most important selection criterion for overseas assignments. However, Industry attaches far greater importance to this criterion than the Consumer group (Table F-3). The Consumer group places greater weight than the Industry group on the selection criteria of "expressed interest" and "prior formal training." Both Industry and Consumer groups stress foreign national status (e.g., a Mexican in Mexico) in the selection criteria.

Both Industry and Consumer groups consider domestic on-the-job training as the most important method of conducting a training program (Table F-4). International on-the-job training is regarded as the second most important method, and is stressed by the Industry group.

Table F-5 shows that the response to the question of who conducts the program is similar between both groups. However, the Industry group places far greater weight on the international marketing group than does the Consumer group.

With respect to the levels at which the program is offered (Table F-6), both groups show a similar response, with Industry stressing the division level.

Integration of international marketing into a unified corporate effort is stressed as a primary objective of the program to a far greater extent by Industry than by the Consumer group (Table F-7). However, both groups consider it important to include in their training programs an overall survey of international marketing.

Table F-8 shows that an increased emphasis on integrating international marketing is viewed as the single most important change expected in the training program. The Consumer group attaches a greater importance to the teaching of sales and distribution techniques than does Industry.

The Industry group expects that their training programs will change to accommodate to the present trend towards the development of an overall international market (Table F-9). In this respect, it shows a significant difference from the Consumer group, which believes that a greater consumer orientation in foreign markets is a far more important reason for changes in the program. It also emphasizes more effective local competition in foreign markets.

Table F-10 shows that both groups consider the teaching of marketing techniques peculiar to overseas operations essential; but Industry stresses in its programs the teaching of "environmental factors" (such as language) and socio-cultural differences.

With respect to the changes expected in the training program, Industry, unlike the Consumer group, places a far greater importance on the trend toward a world customer (Table F-11); however, the Consumer group places a significantly greater importance on empathy. Tables F-9 and F-11 reveal an increasing awareness of social-cultural environmental factors by the Consumer group, but the existing foreign environment training program offered by this group places significantly less emphasis on these aspects than Industry does.

International Marketing Personnel

Both Industry and Consumer groups believe that domestic and international marketing skills are mutually transferable (Table F-12) and that the ability to transfer them depends largely upon the individual. However, mutual transferability is stressed to a significantly greater extent by Industry than by the Consumer group. However, Industry maintains that domestic skills are easily transferable to the international sphere.

Both Industry and Consumer groups consider being out of the corporate mainstream as the most important problem for international marketing personnel (Table F-13). They also stress the difficulties encountered by personnel abroad due to different cultural concepts and values; however, the Industry group places more weight on this point than the Consumer group.

The Industry group considers that a domestic marketing experience is essential for success in international marketing assignments (Table F-14). Although the Consumer group agrees on this point, it considers an empathy with a foreign culture as more important for success. Industry considers an individual's desire to work overseas as a far more important determinant of success in international marketing. Both groups, however, agree that being a national of a country to which one is assigned is also an important determinant of success.

A significant majority of Industry and Consumer groups believe that the present supply of qualified personnel is less than the demand; but a minority in both groups considers the supply to be equal to or greater than the demand (Table F-15).

Also, a significant majority of both Industry and Consumer groups believe that the supply of qualified international marketing personnel will remain less than the demand over the next five years. A minority in both groups (but with a larger representation from Industry) believe that in five years the supply will be equal to the demand (Table F-16).

The major reason for the existing shortage of qualified personnel for both groups is the unwillingness on the part of the candidates to live overseas. Both groups also consider the abstract nature of international marketing as an important reason for the shortage (Table F-17). Again, Table F-18 shows that the reasons accounting for the shortage at present will be primarily responsible for the shortage of qualified personnel over the next five years.

3

OBSERVATIONS: CORPORATE OBJECTIVES,

EMERGING TRENDS, CRITICAL ISSUES

The preceding chapters have dealt with several important aspects of the present state of training for international marketing management with probable future developments. The points presented in this chapter should be considered merely as observations and not as conclusions; much research remains to be done in the field.

SPECIFIC THEMES

The specific themes discussed in this section must be viewed within the context of the broader characteristics affecting international marketing. The extent and nature of the evolution of these themes will depend largely upon the particular characteristics of a company in terms of size, overseas sales, nature of the product, form of overseas operations (subsidiaries, joint ventures), and, most importantly, on the farsightedness of senior management at both the corporate and international division levels.

Integration of International Marketing

Integration of international marketing into a unified, worldwide corporate effort is the most important objective of American companies with international operations. The resurgence of European and Japanese industry is creating an increasing competition for American companies doing business abroad. Besides, competition is becoming more intense among American companies in international operations. Integration of operations is designed to improve the competitive strength of a company.

Senior corporate management is promoting integration at all levels of a company, including that of the international marketing function.[1] The process of integration is resulting in an increasing centralization of strategic decisions (such as product policy and pricing) at corporate headquarters. Thus, new products should be developed with a view to a worldwide market and not only in relation to that of the United States. Of course, the extent and effectiveness of such integration varies by company; however, given the largely domestic orientation of most American companies and of most senior levels of corporate managers, the critical question is whether the integration process is likely to result in imposing the domestic will and way of doing things on ever larger geographic units. The effectiveness of integration will require an awareness on the part of senior corporate executives of the specific and unique characteristics of foreign markets. The cultivation of such sensitivity will be a major task of senior international marketing executives in the future. Failure in this area will increase the probability of senior corporate management underestimating in the process of integration the importance of environmental factors in international marketing.

The process of integration in international marketing raises many serious questions which can not be answered properly at the present. Specifically, in what ways will the overall process of integration affect the role of the international marketing manager? Will it result in his sharing of decisions with non-marketing executives? If so, what effect will it have on the marketing manager's ability to respond quickly and effectively to the dynamic changes taking place in the market place?[2] How should international marketing managers educate the senior levels of corporate management on the unique nature of the international marketing function?

Increasing Uniformity of Markets

The evolution of increasingly uniform markets at the regional level envisioned for the near future will be largely restricted to North America (Canada, United States), Western Europe, and, gradually, Japan. The per capita income, discretionary spending power, level of industrialization —these and other major economic features will become more similar in the future. However, social-cultural factors in these countries will probably remain distinct. For example, in the past, American companies have attempted to transplant, unsuccessfully. food products designed for American tastes into some Western European countries.

The uniformity of markets together with the evolution of corporate integration is likely to result in a uniformity of product development. However, in the process of such development, the international marketing manager will have to make sure that the specific characteristics of a foreign market are incorporated into every new product developed.[3] Accordingly, the training process will have to concentrate on those regional markets which offer increasing economic uniformity but which retain their respective social-cultural characteristics.

The developing countries of Latin America, Asia, Africa, and the Middle East also reflect a certain degree of uniformity in terms of low per capita income, limited discretionary spending power, and low levels of industrialization. It is not unlikely that with respect to these economic criteria, the gap between the developed and the developing countries will increase in the future. On a worldwide basis, a company's markets might be broadly divided between the developed and the developing countries. This characteristic will influence the training of international marketing executives. Thus, the training of executives with responsibilities for developing countries or being assigned to developing countries will emphasize such aspects as host government controls and regulations, economic and political nationalism, and product modification. Particular emphasis might be placed on developing products and marketing programs on a regional basis, such as Southeast Asia or parts of Africa.[4]

As developed countries become more uniform, their absolute size in terms of buying power and, therefore, their importance to a company in terms of percentage of sales will be formidable. As with the danger of extending American ways to Western Europe, a critical question in the future will be the danger by developed countries of imposing ways of doing business on developing countries.

Emphasis on Domestic Skills

A majority of American companies consider a proven domestic marketing ability as the most important determinant of success in international marketing. The reasons are: First, because domestic (United States) sales still account for a significant majority of corporate sales. Second, because during the 1950s and 1960s, when most American companies made their largest overseas investments and sales, the European and other less developed markets were primarily sellers' markets, and the competition faced then was far less than that being experienced at present. Therefore, American companies had little reason to adapt their marketing and general business approaches to achieve a better fit with the locally accepted approaches in a given country.

The strong preference of American companies on domestic experience versus international marketing experience might pose serious problems for corporate development. It is not unlikely that the business concepts and techniques being developed in Western Europe could be relevant for the American context as well. Therefore, the one-way flow of marketing skills reflected by American companies from domestic to international marketing is probably a serious oversight.

The development of worldwide operations, the emergence of multinational enterprises, the process of integration of international operations —these and other major characteristics of the American enterprise require the effective use of foreign nationals. A significant minority of American companies recognize the importance of using foreign nationals in their home country. However, an important characteristic of the international enterprise is the use of foreign nationals in senior managerial positions. This is particularly true in international operations, and in some companies foreign nationals are beginning to occupy senior positions at the corporate level.[5] This trend makes it all the more important to view the transfer of marketing skills as a two-way process, from the domestic to the international and vice versa. To maintain a one-way flow is likely to result in a weakening of the contribution of foreign nationals in top management positions.

An important area for research is that of determining the extent and the manner in which international marketing skills can be better appreciated and understood for their relevance to the United States context. This point is of particular significance to the current crop of junior and middle management executives being groomed for the larger responsibilities of a worldwide market.

Educating Corporate Executives

Given the largely domestic orientation of the senior levels of corporate management, international marketing managers are faced with the important task of educating senior management on the characteristics of international business operations. Some of the large, and many of the giant American companies, especially those with significant overseas sales, are familiar with the special requirements for successful international operations. However, the senior executives of many of the small- and medium-size companies included in this study do not have a sufficient understanding of international business which is essential for a successful penetration of foreign markets.

Senior corporate managers should be thoroughly familiar with career development and environmental understanding. A handicap resulting from international assignments is that of isolating executives from the corporate mainstream. An executive assigned to a foreign market often believes that he is at a disadvantage either because he is away from the key positions at promotion time or because senior management underestimates the importance of his skills in international business operations. An international assignment is usually not counted towards a promotion in the corporate hierarchy. Thus, international marketing will be at a serious disadvantage in attracting people of high caliber unless senior corporate executives attach greater importance to the skills required in managing international business operations.

A second important educational task is to increase the understanding by senior corporate executives of environmental factors in foreign countries. Yet, it is just those environmental factors which are difficult for senior corporate executives to fully understand or accept; given the importance of such factors for international marketing, the effectiveness of the management training program will be significantly determined by the extent to which it effectively orients senior corporate executives.

Environmental Training

A major reason for the failure of international marketing personnel is an improper understanding of socio-cultural and other factors relating to a foreign environment. Yet, the training programs offer very limited exposure to such environmental factors. The largely domestic orientation and the presence of essentially sellers' markets in the past have been the primary reasons for this shortcoming. However, because of the reasons dealt with in the preceding sections, the international markets of the 1970s and beyond will require a far greater degree of environmental understanding on the part of all international executives, in particular of those with international marketing responsibilities.

*   *   *

Compared to other functions—such as accounting, production, and finance—the marketing function is unique. It interacts constantly with customers—the people—in the marketplace. Through marketing, the company must anticipate, recognize, research, create, and deliver a product effectively to the consumers at a profit acceptable to the company. Given this key characteristic of marketing, the nature and content of the training program must deal with subjects which might not be considered essential in programs of accounting and finance.[6]

International marketing is a part of international business operations, itself a strategy for overall corporate evolution. The themes reflected in this book must be viewed within the much larger corporate context which might encourage or inhibit their development. The effectiveness of training programs for international marketing management, for example, will depend on the ability of key executives to anticipate and to influence the nature of broader corporate forces.

The international marketing function is evolving many new characteristics as a result of various changes within corporations and the environment of international markets. The themes dealt with here are of utmost importance to the emerging generation of executives and to their effective performance in international marketing positions. Ways and means must be found to express meaningfully these themes in the training process.

APPENDIXES

A P P E N D I X A

SAMPLE DESIGN

The mailing list was compiled from the *Fortune 500* of 1969, with a specific executive as the addressee for each of the 384 firms. The executive chosen was either the senior international executive, the senior marketing executive, or the president. This census of international firms in the "500" should provide a good cross section of the criteria employed for the selection of trainees in international marketing.

Verification of overseas activity was based on three sources:

a)   the July 1969 edition of *Moody's Industrial Manual;*

b)   the 1970 edition of *Poor's Register of Corporations, Directors, and Executives;*

c)   the 1969 edition of the *Directory of American Firms Operating in Foreign Countries (7th ed.)*

38

A P P E N D I X   B

THE TRAINING OF INTERNATIONAL MARKETING MANAGERS:

A QUESTIONNAIRE SURVEY*

[*At times the response of companies did not match the choices
offered in the questionnaire.   In some   cases, a sufficiently
large number of responses to problems not   originally included
in the questionnaire justified a new category of tabulation.]

I   GENERAL BACKGROUND

1. What were the *approximate total sales* of your firm in 1969?

    ___ $150 - $200 million   ___ $401 - $600 million
    ___ $201 - $300 million   ___ $601 - $1,000 million
    ___ $301 - $400 million   ___ $1,001 - $2,000 million
                                     ___ over $2,000 million

2. Approximately what *percent* of these sales were *from foreign operations?*

    ___ 0 - 10%   ___ 51 - 75%
    ___ 11 - 25%   ___ over 75%
    ___ 26 - 50%

3. What *major product line or service* does your firm market abroad?

    _____

4. What is the *primary market* for that product or service?

    ___ industry   ___ consumer
    ___ government   ___ other (please describe)_____

5. What are your firm's *major international marketing problem areas?*   (Please rank 1, 2, etc. in order of importance)

    ___ increasing nationalism abroad reflected in consumer
            practices
    ___ unsuitable channels of distribution
    ___ unfair competition from foreign government and/or
            foreign enterprises
    ___ lack of marketing information and data
    ___ lack of marketing support services such as advertising
    ___ product adaptation to local (foreign) use
    ___ integration of international marketing into a
            unified, world-wide corporate marketing
            effort
    ___ other (please describe)_____

6. In what ways is *international marketing different*
    from domestic marketing in your firm?   (Please rank
    1, 2, etc. in order of importance)

    ___ greater emphasis on consumer orientation in
            domestic
    ___ greater government regulation in international
    ___ greater need for additional data in international
    ___ greater need for more feedback and control in
            international
    ___ lesser awareness of international problems by top
            corporate management
    ___ greater need to integrate international marketing
            at corporate level
    ___ greater need to integrate international marketing
            at division level
    ___ no significant difference between the two
    ___ other (please describe)_____

II THE INTERNATIONAL MARKETING TRAINING PROGRAM

7. How do you *select personnel* for positions in interna-
        tional marketing? (Please rank 1, 2, etc. in
        order of importance)

    ___ those expressing interest in international
            marketing
    ___ those with prior formal training in the field,
            e.g., college
    ___ those with foreign language ability
    ___ those with proven domestic marketing ability
    ___ those being prepared for eventual greater
            responsibility in the U. S.
    ___ other (please describe)_____

8. What *methods are used in conducting* your international
        marketing training program? (Please rank 1, 2, etc.
        in order of importance)

    ___ domestic on-the-job training
    ___ overseas on-the-job training
    ___ formal program conducted by company
    ___ formal program conducted by outside agency
    ___ seminar type course on an *ad hoc* basis
    ___ other (please describe) _____

9. Who *conducts* the program? (Please rank 1, 2, etc. in order of importance)

  ___ marketing department
  ___ international division
  ___ international marketing group
  ___ functional supervisor
  ___ professional association, e.g., American Management Association
  ___ college or university
  ___ other (please describe)_____

10. At *what levels* of the organization are international marketing training *programs offered?*

  ___ corporate level
  ___ division level
  ___ regional level (including two or more countries)
  ___ individual country level
  ___ all levels
  ___ no internally administered programs are offered
  ___ other (please describe)_____

11. What are the *primary objectives* of your international marketing training program? (Please rank 1, 2, etc. in order of importance)

  ___ to offer an overall survey of the general aspects of international marketing
  ___ to stress the concrete characteristics of international marketing such as greater government regulation, lesser data, etc.
  ___ to demonstrate the abstract differences compared to domestic marketing, e.g., lesser consumer orientation found abroad
  ___ to emphasize importance of integration of international marketing into a unified, world-wide corporate marketing effort
  ___ other (please describe)_____

12. What *changes* do you expect in your international marketing training program *within the next five years?* (Please rank 1, 2, etc. in order of importance)

___ greater emphasis on product adaptability
___ greater emphasis on sales and distribution
    techniques
___ greater emphasis on such characteristics as
    language and local business customs
___ greater emphasis on socio-political aspects
    such as nationalism
___ greater emphasis on integrating international
    marketing into a world-wide corporate effort
___ other (please describe)_____

13. *Why* do you feel the *changes* you indicated above *will
    occur?* (Please rank 1, 2, etc. in order of
    importance)

    ___ more sophisticated products will be introduced
        on a larger scale into less developed
        countries
    ___ greater consumer orientation will occur in
        foreign markets

    ___ greater cooperation with local partners and
        middle-men will develop
    ___ local enterprises will provide more effective
        and vigorous competition
    ___ an overall international market rather than
        several foreign markets will begin to
        develop
    ___ other (please describe) _____

14. What aspects of *foreign environment training* are in-
    cluded in your international marketing training
    program? (Please rank 1, 2, etc. in order of
    importance)

    ___ specifics such as language, regulatory climate,
        local business traits, etc.
    ___ concepts such as the understanding of social
        and cultural differences
    ___ emphasis on marketing techniques peculiar to
        overseas operations, e.g., differences in
        channels of distribution
    ___ other (please describe) _____

15. Do you feel that the *foreign environment training* part
     of your program will *change* significantly within
     the next five years and, if so, why? (Please
     rank 1, 2, etc. in order of importance)

___ trend to consumer orientation will demand
    greater empathy
___ increased product sophistication will require
    greater product knowledge
___ local business will provide more effective
    competition requiring greater consumer
    identification
___ trend to a world customer rather than indivi-
    dual foreign markets will be apparent
___ no change in this part of program anticipated
___ other (please describe) _____

III INTERNATIONAL MARKETING PERSONNEL

16. Do you believe that international and domestic *market-
     ing skills* are *transferable?* (Please rank 1, 2,
     etc. in order of importance)

___ domestic skills transferable to international
___ international skills transferable to domestic
___ neither transferable
___ mutually transferable
___ depends on the individual
___ other (please describe) _____

17. What are the main *difficulties faced* by your inter-
     national marketing *personnel?* (Please rank 1, 2,
     etc. in order of importance)

___ adapting to different standards of living
___ overcoming language barrier
___ adapting to different cultural concepts
___ being out of corporate "mainstream"
___ other (please describe) _____

18. What *characteristics favor success* in international marketing personnel? (Please rank 1, 2, etc. in order of importance)

___ foreign language ability
___ strong empathy with foreign social-cultural environment
___ domestic marketing experience
___ desire to work overseas
___ college or university training
___ corporate international marketing training
___ being a national of the country to which assigned
___ other (please describe) _____

19. What is the *supply of international marketing personnel* with those qualifications you listed in the preceding question?

Today	*In Five Years*	
_____	_____	supply greater than demand
_____	_____	supply less than demand
_____	_____	supply equal to demand

20. What do you believe *causes shortage of international marketing personnel?* (Please rank 1, 2, etc. in order of importance)

Today	*In Five Years*	
_____	_____	unwillingness to live abroad
_____	_____	lack of college level programs
_____	_____	abstract nature of international marketing
_____	_____	no shortage noted
_____	_____	other (please describe) _____

Thank you very much for your help in this project, We
would be interested in learning your *firm's name* and
your title although these two items are *optional.*

    Firm Name _____

    Respondent's Title _____

If you are interested in learning of the findings of
this study, we will gladly send you a copy of the results
when available. Please indicate to whom they should be
sent.

    Name _____

    Address _____

       _____

A P P E N D I X   C

RESPONSES ACCORDING TO INTERNATIONAL SALES AND FIRM SIZE

1. *MAJOR INTERNATIONAL MARKETING PROBLEMS*

International Sales	Small	Medium	Large	Giant	Response
Small					No Response
Medium				1	
Large				1	
Small		2	1		Increasing Nation-
Medium		1		1	alism
Large		1			
Small		3	1	1	Unsuitable Channels
Medium	3		3		of Distribution
Large	1		2		
Small	1	2			Unfair Competition
Medium		1		2	
Large		1	2	1	
Small	2	2	1		Lack of Marketing
Medium	2	1	7		Data
Large			2	1	
Small	1	2	4		Trade Barriers
Medium		2	2		
Large		1			
Small	2		2		Product Adaptation
Medium					to Foreign Use
Large	1				
Small	3	2	2		Integration of
Medium	5	2	4	1	International
Large		2	5	2	Marketing
Small				1	Other, or Multiple
Medium				1	Unranked
Large				1	Responses
Small	2	3			Shortage of Quali-
Medium	1	3			fied Personnel
Large					
Small	1	3	1		Local Legal and
Medium	1		2		Political Com-
Large	1				plications

2. *DOMESTIC AND INTERNATIONAL MARKETING DIFFERENCES*

International Sales	Size of Firm				Response
	Small	*Medium*	*Large*	*Giant*	
Small					No Response
Medium	2				
Large					
Small		1	1	1	Domestic Consumer
Medium		1			Orientation
Large					
Small	3	2	4		More Government
Medium	2	3	4	1	Regulation in
Large	2	2	3	2	International
Small		2	1		Need for More Data
Medium	1		4		in International
Large			1		
World				1	
Small		2	1		Need for More Feed-
Medium	3	2		2	back and Control in
Large	1	1	1	1	International
Small	3	3	2		Top Management's
Medium		2	2		Lesser Awareness of
Large	1		1		International Problems
Small	3		1		Need to Integrate
Medium	1	1			International
Large			1		Marketing at Corporate Level
Small	1	1			Need to Integrate
Medium	2	2	3		International Marketing at Division Level
Large				1	
Small		2	1		No Significant
Medium	2		1	2	Difference
Large	1	2	4		
Small		3	1	1	Other, or Multiple
Medium			2	1	Unranked Responses
Large	2	1		1	

3. PERSONNEL SELECTION CRITERIA

International Sales	Size of Firm				Response
	Small	Medium	Large	Giant	
Small		1			No Response
Medium	1		1		
Large					
Small	2	4	3		Expressed Interest
Medium		4	3		in International
Large		1		1	Marketing
Small	1	2	1		Prior Formal
Medium	1	1	2	1	Training
Large	2		1		
Small		1			Foreign Language
Medium	1				Ability
Large					
Small	4	3	4	1	Proven Domestic
Medium	7	4	9	3	Marketing Ability
Large	2	3	3	2	
World				1	
Small		3	1		Those Being Pre-
Medium					pared For Greater
Large			2		Domestic Respon-
					sibility
Small	3	2	3	1	Foreign National
Medium	3	2	1	2	Status
Large	3	2	5	2	

4. METHOD OF CONDUCTING TRAINING PROGRAM

International Sales	Small	Medium	Large	Giant	Response
Small		2			No Response
Medium	1		1		
Large					
Small	5	6	7	1	Domestic on-the-
Medium	6	4	10	3	job Training
Large	3	3	1	1	
Small	4	3	3	1	International on-
Medium	4	5	3	2	the-job Training
Large	1	2	7	1	
World				1	
Small			2		Formal Company
Medium	2	2			Program
Large	2		1	2	
Small		1			Formal Outside
Medium					Program
Large					
Small	1				Seminar-type
Medium					Courses on an *ad*
Large					*hoc* Basis
Small		4			Other, or Multiple
Medium			2	1	Unranked Responses
Large	1	1	2	1	

5. WHO CONDUCTS THE PROGRAM

International Sales	Size of Firm				Response
	Small	*Medium*	*Large*	*Giant*	
Small		3		1	No Response
Medium	1		2	1	
Large					
Small		4	1	1	Marketing Department
Medium	1	2	2		
Large	3	2		1	
Small	6	4	4		International
Medium	5	5	4	2	Division
Large	3	1	5		
Small	3	3	6		International
Medium	2	2	3	2	Marketing Group
Large		2	2	1	
Small	1	1	1		Functional Supervisor
Medium	2	2	2	1	
Large			3	2	
World				1	
Small					Professional
Medium					Association
Large				1	
Small		1			Other, or Multiple
Medium	2		3		Unranked Responses
Large	1	1	1		

6, LEVELS AT WHICH PROGRAM IS OFFERED

International Sales	Size of Firm				Response
	Small	*Medium*	*Large*	*Giant*	
Small		3			No Response
Medium	1		1	2	
Large			1		
Small		1	1		Corporate Level
Medium					
Large		1	1		
Small	3	5	7		Division Level
Medium	3	5	7		
Large	3	1	1		
Small	2				Regional Levels
Medium	2	3	1		
Large					
Small		1			Individual Countries
Medium	1	1	2		
Large			2		
Small		5	1		All Levels
Medium		2	2	1	
Large	3		4	2	
Small	2		2	1	No Internal Programs
Medium	2				
Large		3	2	1	
World				1	
Small	2	1	2	1	Where Needed or No Particular Level
Medium	4		2	4	
Large	1	1	1	1	

7.PRIMARY OBJECTIVES OF PROGRAM

International Sales	Size of Firm				Response
	Small	Medium	Large	Giant	
Small	3	5	1	1	No Response
Medium	3		1	1	
Large				2	
World				1	
Small	2	4	4		General Survey of
Medium	4	5	3	1	International
Large	1	1	4	1	Marketing
Small	2		1	1	Stress the Concrete
Medium	2	1		2	Characteristics
Large				1	
Small	2		2		Demonstrate the
Medium					Abstract Features
Large					
Small	1	6	2		Emphasize the
Medium	2	1	7	1	Corporate Inte-
Large	2	2	3		gration of Inter-
					national Marketing
Small		1	1		Other, or Multiple
Medium	2		1		Unranked Responses
Large	4		1		
Small	1			1	Impart Specific
Medium		3	1		Product & Selling
Large		1	2	1	Knowledge
Small					Cultural Sensi-
Medium		1	3	1	tization
Large		1	1		

8. EXPECTED CHANGES IN THE TRAINING PROGRAM

International Sales	Size of Firm				Response
	Small	*Medium*	*Large*	*Giant*	
Small	1	2	1	1	No Response
Medium	2			1	
Large	2			3	
Small	1	1	4		Increased Emphasis
Medium	2	1	2	2	on Product Adapt-
Large	1	1			ability
Small	4	6	2		Increased Emphasis
Medium	6	3		2	on Sales and Dis-
Large	2	2	1	1	tribution Techniques
Small					Increased Emphasis
Medium	1	1	1		on Local Variations
Large			1		Such as Language
Small			1	1	Increased Emphasis
Medium		1		1	on Socio-political
Large					Aspects
Small	4	4	4		Increased Emphasis
Medium	2	4	11		on Corporate Inte-
Large	1	1	6	2	gration of Inter- national Marketing
Small		3			Structural Changes
Medium		1	2		Such as Introduction
Large	1	2	3		of Formal Training Programs

9. REASONS FOR EXPECTED CHANGES IN PROGRAM

| International Sales | Size of Firm | | | | Response |
Sales	*Small*	*Medium*	*Large*	*Giant*	
Small	1	3	1	1	No Response
Medium	2	1		1	
Large				2	
World				1	
Small	3	2	3		Introduction of
Medium	6	1	2	1	More Sophisticated
Large	1				Products Into Less
					Developed Areas
Small	3	1	1		Greater Consumer
Medium	1	1	3		Orientation
Large	1	1	1	2	Developing Abroad
Small		1	2	1	Greater Cooperation
Medium		1	1		With Local Interests
Large		1	1	1	
Small		2	3		More Effective Local
Medium	3	2	1	3	Competition
Large	1	2	2		
Small	2	7	1		Development of Over-
Medium	1	5	8		all World Market
Large	1	2	6	1	Concept
Small		2			Other, or Multiple
Medium		1	1		Unranked Responses
Large		1	2		

10. FOREIGN ENVIRONMENT TRAINING

International Sales	Size of Firm				Response
	Small	*Medium*	*Large*	*Giant*	
Small	2	2	1	1	No Response
Medium	3	1	1		
Large	1		1	1	
Small	1	3	3		Specifics Such as
Medium	4	2	3		Language, Regulatory
Large		1		1	Climate, etc.
Small		1			Concepts Such as
Medium		1			Cultural Differences
Large			4		
Small	6	10	7	1	Marketing Techniques
Medium	5	8	10	5	Peculiar to Overseas
Large	6	4	4	3	Operations
Small	1		1		Other, or Multiple
Medium	1		2	1	Unranked Responses
Large	1		2		

11. EXPECTED CHANGES IN FOREIGN ENVIRONMENT TRAINING

International Sales	Size of Firm				Response
	Small	*Medium*	*Large*	*Giant*	
Small	2	2	2	1	No Response
Medium	4	2	2	1	
Large		1	1	2	
Small	2	1			Greater Emphasis
Medium	1	1	3	1	on Consumer Empathy
Large	2			1	
Small	2	4	4		Emphasis on Greater
Medium	1	3	1	1	Product Knowledge
Large	2	2	1		Due to Increased Product Sophistication
Small		2	2		Emphasis on Consumer
Medium	2		1	3	Identification Due
Large			1	1	to Better Local Competition
Small	2	1	1		Trend to a World
Medium	2	2	5		Customer Concept
Large	1		4	1	Will Develop
Small	2	5	3	1	No Change
Medium	3	3	3		
Large		2	3	1	
Small		1			Other, or Multiple
Medium			1		Unranked Responses
Large	2	1	1		

12. TRANSFERABILITY OF MARKETING SKILLS

| International Sales | Size of Firm | | | | Response |
	Small	Medium	Large	Giant	
Small	1	3	3	1	Domestic Skills
Medium		2	4	4	Transferable to
Large	3	1	2	2	International
Small		1			International
Medium		1	1	1	Skills Transferable
Large					to Domestic
Small		1			Neither Trans-
Medium					ferable
Large	1		1		
Small	4	2	2		Skills Are Mutu-
Medium	9	4	6		ally Transferable
Large	1	3	6	3	
Small	5	7	7	1	Transferability
Medium	4	4	4		Depends on the
Large	2	2	1	2	Individual
Small		2			Other, or Multiple
Medium			1	1	Unranked Responses
Large					

13. DIFFICULTIES CONFRONTING INTERNATIONAL MARKETING PERSONNEL

International Sales	Small	Medium	Large	Giant	Responses
Small	1			2	No Response
Medium	2				
Large					
Small	2	5			Different Standards
Medium	1	4	3	1	of Living
Large			2	2	
Small		1	2	1	Language Barrier
Medium	1				
Large		3	2		
Small	3	2	5	1	Different Cul-
Medium	4	6	7	1	tural Concepts
Large	5	2	1	2	
Small	4	9	5		Being Out of the
Medium	5	2	7		Corporate Main-
Large			4	1	stream
Small			1		Other, or Multiple
Medium			1	1	Unranked Responses
Large				2	

14. CHARACTERISTICS FAVORING SUCCESS
IN INTERNATIONAL MARKETING PERSONNEL

International Sales	Size of Firm				Response
	Small	*Medium*	*Large*	*Giant*	
Small		1			No Response
Medium			1		
Large					
Small	1	1	1		Foreign Language
Medium			1		Ability
Large					
Small	1	6	1	1	Strong Empathy
Medium	3	4	5	1	With Foreign
Large	2	2	1	1	Environment
Small	1	4	2	1	Domestic Market-
Medium	5		6	2	ing Experience
Large		3	1	1	
Small		4	2		Desire to Work
Medium	2		2	1	Overseas
Large	1		1		
World				1	
Small	1		2		College or Uni-
Medium					versity Training
Large	1				
Small	1				Corporate Inter-
Medium	1	2			national Marketing
Large	1		1	1	Training
Small	3		3		Being a National
Medium	1	3		2	of Country to Which
Large	1		4	1	Assigned
Small	2		1		Other, or Multiple
Medium	1	2	1		Unranked Responses
Large	1	1	3	1	

15. SUPPLY OF INTERNATIONAL MARKETING PERSONNEL TODAY

International Sales	Size of Firm				Response
	Small	*Medium*	*Large*	*Giant*	
Small		3			No Response
Medium	1				
Large					
Small	2	5	2	1	Supply Greater
Medium				2	Than Demand
Large				1	
World				1	
Small	7	7	8		Supply Less
Medium	10	8	12	2	Than Demand
Large	5	5	7	2	
Small	1	1	2	1	Supply Equal
Medium	2	3	4	2	to Demand
Large	2	1	4	2	

*16. SUPPLY OF INTERNATIONAL
MARKETING PERSONNEL WITHIN FIVE YEARS*

International Sales	Size of Firm				Response
	Small	*Medium*	*Large*	*Giant*	
Small	1	2			No Response
Medium	1				
Large					
Small	1	2	2	1	Supply Greater
Medium				1	Than Demand
Large	1		1		
World				1	
Small	5	10	6		Supply Less
Medium	11	7	8	1	Than Demand
Large	4	4	9	3	
Small	3	2	4	1	Supply Equal
Medium	1	4	8	4	to Demand
Large	2	2	1	2	

l7. CAUSES OF CURRENT SHORTAGE OF QUALIFIED PERSONNEL

International Sales	Size of Firm				Response
	Small	*Medium*	*Large*	*Giant*	
Small	2	4	1		No Response
Medium	1		1	1	
Large			1		
World				1	
Small	1	2	3		Unwillingness
Medium	4	2	2	1	to Live Abroad
Large	1	1	1	2	
Small					Lack of College
Medium	2		1		Level Programs
Large	1		1		
Small	2	2	3		Abstract Nature
Medium		4	3		of International
Large	1	1	2		Marketing
Small	1	4	1	2	No Shortage
Medium	1	1	3	3	
Large	2	1	1	2	
Small	4	4	4		Other, or Multiple
Medium	5	4	6	1	Unranked Responses
Large	2	3	5	1	

18. CAUSES OF FUTURE SHORTAGE OF QUALIFIED PERSONNEL

International Sales	Size of Firm				Response
	Small	*Medium*	*Large*	*Giant*	
Small	4	6	4		No Response
Medium	5	1	2	2	
Large			3	1	
World				1	
Small	1	3	3		Unwillingness
Medium	3	2	3	1	to Live Abroad
Large	1	1	3	1	
Small					Lack of College
Medium	1				Level Programs
Large					
Small	2	2	1		Abstract Nature
Medium		3	3	1	of International
Large	1		1	1	Marketing
Small			2	2	No Shortage
Medium	1	1	5	2	Expected
Large	3	2		1	
Small	3	3	2		Other, or Multiple
Medium	3	4	3		Unranked Responses
Large	2	3	4	1	

APPENDIX D

RESPONSES ACCORDING TO FIRM SIZE ONLY

Major International Marketing Problems	Size of Firm			
	Small	Medium	Large	Giant
Local Legal and Political Complications	3	3	3	
Increasing Nationalism		4	1	1
Unsuitable Channels	4	3	6	1
Unfair Competition	1	4	2	3
Lack of Data	4	3	10	1
Lack of Support Services				
Product Adaptation	3		2	
Integration of International Marketing	8	6	11	3
Other/Multiple Unranked				3
No Response				2
Trade Barriers	1	5	6	
Scarcity of Personnel	3	6		

Domestic and International Marketing Differences	Small	Medium	Large	Giant
Domestic Consumer Orientation		2	1	1
Greater International Regulation	7	7	11	3
Need for More Data -- International	1	2	6	1
Need for More Feedback/ Control International	4	5	2	3
Less Awareness of International Problems by Top Management	4	5	5	
Need to Integrate International Marketing at Corporate Level	4	1	2	
at Division Level	3	3	3	1
No Difference	3	4	6	2
Other/Multiple Unranked	2	4	3	3
No Response	2			

Personnel Selection Criteria	Small	Medium	Large	Giant
Expressed Interest	2	9	6	1
Prior Formal Training	4	3	4	1
Foreign Language Ability	1	1		
Domestic Marketing Ability	13	10	16	7
Preparation For Greater Domestic Responsibility		3	3	
Foreign National Status	9	6	9	5
No Response	1	1	1	

Method of Conducting Program	Size of Firm			
	Small	*Medium*	*Large*	*Giant*
Domestic on-the-job Training	14	13	18	5
International on-the-job Training	9	10	13	5
Formal Corporate Program	4	2	3	2
Formal Outside Program		1		
Seminar Type Courses	1			
Other/Multiple Unranked	1	5	4	2
No Response	1	2	1	

Who Conducts Program				
Marketing Department	4	8	3	2
International Division	14	10	13	2
International Marketing Group	5	7	11	3
Functional Supervisor	3	3	6	4
Professional Association				1
College/University				
Other/Multiple Unranked	3	2	4	
No Response	1	3	2	2

Levels at Which Program is Offered				
Corporate		2	2	
Division	9	11	15	
Regional	4	3	1	
Individual Country	1	2	4	
All Levels	3	7	7	3
No Internal Programs	4	3	4	3
No Response	1	3	2	2
Where Needed	7	2	5	6

Program Primary Objective				
Overall Survey	7	10	11	2
Stress Concrete Characteristics	4	1	1	4
Demonstrate Abstract Differences	2		2	
Integration of International Marketing Within Firm	5	9	12	1
Other/Multiple Unranked	6	1	3	
No Response	6	5	2	5
Impart Specific Product and Selling Knowledge	1	4	4	1
Cultural Sensitization		2	4	1

Expected Changes in Program	Size of Firm			
	Small	*Medium*	*Large*	*Giant*
Increased Emphasis on Product Adaptability	4	3	6	2
Increased Emphasis on Sales and Distribution Techniques	12	11	3	3
Increased Emphasis on Local Variations, e.g. Language	1	1	2	
Increased Emphasis on Socio-Political Aspects		1	1	2
Increased Emphasis on Integrating International Marketing	7	9	21	2
No Response	5	2	1	5
Structural Changes Such as Introduction of Formal Training Programs	1	6	5	

Reason for Change				
Introduction of More Sophisticated Products	10	3	5	1
Greater Consumer Orientation	5	3	5	2
Greater Cooperation With Local Interests		3	4	2
More Effective Local Competition	4	6	6	3
Development of Overall International Market	4	14	15	1
Other/Multiple Unranked		4	3	
No Response	3	4	1	5

Foreign Environment Training				
Specifics Such as Language	5	6	6	1
Concepts Such as Socio-Cultural Differences		2	4	
Marketing Techniques Peculiar to Overseas Operations	17	22	21	9
Other/Multiple Unranked	3		5	1
No Response	5	3	3	3

Expected Changes				
Greater Stress on Empathy	5	2	3	2
Greater Stress on Product Knowledge	5	9	6	1
Greater Stress on Consumer Identification	2	2	4	4
Trend to World Customer	5	3	10	1
No Change	5	10	9	2
Other/Multiple Unranked	2	2	2	
No Response	6	5	5	4

Transferability of Marketing Skills	Size of Firm			
	Small	*Medium*	*Large*	*Giant*
Domestic Transferable to International	4	6	9	7
International Transferable to Domestic		2	1	1
Neither Transferable	1	1	1	
Mutually Transferable	14	9	14	3
Depends on Individual	11	13	13	2
Other/Multiple Unranked		2	1	1

Difficulties Facing International Marketing Personnel				
Different Standard of Living	3	9	5	3
Language Barrier	1	4	4	1
Different Cultural Concepts	12	10	13	4
Being Out of Corporate Mainstream	9	11	16	1
Other/Multiple Unranked			2	3
No Response	3			2

Characteristics Favoring Success				
Foreign Language Ability	1	1	2	
Empathy With Foreign Environment	6	12	7	3
Domestic Marketing Experience	6	7	9	4
Desire To Work Overseas	3	4	5	2
College/University Training	2		2	
Corporate International Marketing Training	3	2	1	1
Being National of Country To Which Assigned	5	3	7	3
Other/Multiple Unranked	4	3	5	1
No Response		1	1	

Supply of Qualified Personnel Today				
Greater Than Demand	2	5	2	5
Less Than Demand	22	20	27	4
Equal To Demand	5	5	10	5
No Response	1	3		

Supply of Qualified Person- nel Within Five Years	Size of Firm			
	Small	*Medium*	*Large*	*Giant*
Greater Than Demand	2	2	3	3
Less Than Demand	20	21	23	4
Equal to Demand	6	8	13	7
No Response	2	2		

Cause of Shortage Today

	Small	*Medium*	*Large*	*Giant*
Unwillingness to Live Abroad	6	5	6	3
Lack of College Level Programs	3		2	
Abstract Nature of Inter- national Marketing	3	7	8	
No Shortage	4	6	5	7
Other/Multiple Unranked	11	11	15	2
No Response	2	2	4	4

Cause of Shortage Within
Five Years

	Small	*Medium*	*Large*	*Giant*
Unwillingness to Live Abroad	5	6	9	2
Lack of College Level Programs	1			
Abstract Nature of Inter- national Marketing	3	5	5	2
No Shortage	4	5	7	5
Other/Multiple Unranked	8	10	9	1
No Response	9	7	9	4

APPENDIX E

RESPONSES ACCORDING TO INTERNATIONAL SALES ONLY

Major International Marketing Problem	International Sales		
	Small	*Medium*	*Large*
Local Legal and Political Complications	5	3	1
Increasing Nationalism	3	2	1
Unsuitable Distribution Channels	5	6	3
Unfair Competition	3	3	4
Lack of Marketing Data	5	10	3
Lack of Marketing Support Services			
Product Adaptation	4		1
Integration of International Marketing	7	12	9
Other/Multiple Unranked	1	1	1
No Response		12	1
Trade Barriers	7	4	1
Scarcity of Personnel	5	4	

Domestic and International Marketing Differences			
Domestic Consumer Orientation	3	1	
Greater International Regulation	9	10	9
Need for More Data -- International	3	5	1
Need for More Feedback/Control -- International	3	7	4
Less Awareness of International Problems by Top Management	8	4	2
Need to Integrate International Marketing at Corporate Level	4	2	1
at Division Level	2	7	1
No Difference	3	5	7
Other/Multiple Unranked	5	3	4
No Response			2

Personnel Selection Criteria			
Expressed Interest	9	7	2
Prior Formal Training	4	5	3
Foreign Language Ability	1	1	
Domestic Marketing Ability	12	23	10
Preparation for Greater Domestic Responsibility	4		2
Foreign National Status	9	8	12
No Response	1	2	

Method of Conducting Program	International Sales		
	Small	Medium	Large
Domestic on-the-job Training	19	23	8
International on-the-job Training	11	14	12
Formal Corporate Program	2	4	5
Formal Outside Program	1		
Seminar Type Courses	1		
Other/Multiple Unranked	4	3	5
No Response	2	2	

Who Conducts Program			
Marketing Department	6	5	6
International Division	14	16	9
International Marketing Group	12	9	5
Functional Supervisor	3	7	6
Professional Association			1
College/University			
Other/Multiple Unranked	1	5	3
No Response	4	4	

Levels at Which Program is Offered			
Corporate	2		2
Division	15	15	5
Regional	2	6	
Individual Country	1	4	2
All Levels	6	5	9
No Internal Programs	5	2	7
No Response	3	4	1
Where Needed or No Particular Level	6	10	4

Program Primary Objective			
Overall Survey	10	13	7
Stress Concrete Characteristics	4	5	1
Demonstrate Abstract Differences	4		
Integration of International Marketing Within Firm	9	11	7
Other/Multiple Unranked	1	1	1
No Response	10	5	3
Impart Specific Product and Selling Knowledge	2	4	4
Cultural Sensitization		5	2

Expected Changes in Program	International Sales		
	Small	*Medium*	*Large*
Increased Emphasis on Product Adaptability	6	7	2
Increased Emphasis on Sales and Distribution Techniques	2	11	6
Increased Emphasis on Local Variations, e.g., Language		3	1
Increased Emphasis on Socio-Political Aspects	2	2	10
Increased Emphasis on Integrating International Marketing	12	17	10
No Response	5	3	5
Structural Changes Such as Introduction of Formal Training Program	3	3	6

Reason for Change

Introduction of More Sophisticated Products	8	10	1
Greater Consumer Orientation	5	5	5
Greater Cooperation With Local Interests	4	2	3
More Effective Local Competition	5	9	5
Development of Overall International Market	10	14	10
Other/Multiple Unranked	2	2	3
No Response	6	4	3

Foreign Environment Training

Specifics Such as Language	7	9	2
Concepts Such as Socio-Cultural Differences	1	1	4
Marketing Techniques Peculiar to Overseas Operations	24	28	17
Other/Multiple Unranked	2	4	3
No Response	6	4	3

Expected Changes

Greater Stress on Empathy	3	6	3
Greater Stress on Product Knowledge	10	6	5
Greater Stress on Consumer Identification	4	6	2
Trend to World Customer	4	9	6
No Change	11	9	6
Other/Multiple Unranked	1	1	4
No Response	7	9	4

Transferability of Marketing Skills	International Sales		
	Small	*Medium*	*Large*
Domestic Transferable to International	8	10	8
International Transferable to Domestic	1	3	
Neither Transferable	1		2
Mutually Transferable	8	19	13
Depends on Individual	20	12	7
Other/Multiple Unranked	2	2	

Difficulties Facing International Marketing Personnel			
Different Standard of Living	8	9	4
Language Barrier	4	1	5
Different Cultural Concepts	11	18	10
Being Out of Corporate Mainstream	18	14	5
Other/Multiple Unranked	1	2	2
No Response	1	4	

Characteristics Favoring Success			
Foreign Language Ability	3	1	
Empathy With Foreign Environment	9	13	6
Domestic Marketing Experience	8	13	5
Desire to Work Overseas	6	5	1
College/University Training	3		1
Corporate International Marketing Training	1	3	3
Being National of Country to Which Assigned	6	6	6
Other/Multiple Unranked	3	4	6
No Response	1	1	

Supply of Qualified Personnel Today			
Greater Than Demand	10	2	2
Less Than Demand	22	32	19
Equal to Demand	5	11	9
No Response	3	1	

Supply of Qualified Personnel
Within Five Years

	International Sales		
	Small	Medium	Large
Greater Than Demand	6	1	3
Less Than Demand	21	27	20
Equal to Demand	10	17	7
No Response	3	1	

Cause of Shortage Today

	Small	Medium	Large
Unwillingness to Live Abroad	6	9	5
Lack of College Level Programs		3	2
Abstract Nature of International Marketing	7	7	4
No Shortage	8	8	6
Other/Multiple Unranked	12	16	11
No Response	7	3	2

Cause of Shortage Within
Five Years

	Small	Medium	Large
Unwillingness to Live Abroad	7	9	6
Lack of College Level Programs		1	
Abstract Nature of International Marketing	5	7	3
No Shortage	6	9	6
Other/Multiple Unranked	8	10	10
No Response	14	10	5

APPENDIX F

RESPONSES ACCORDING TO PRIMARY CUSTOMER ONLY

1. Major International
   Marketing Problem

	Primary Customer		
	Industry	Consumer	Other
Local Legal and Political Complications	4	3	2
Increasing Nationalism	5		1
Unsuitable Distribution Channels	6	7	1
Unfair Competition	5	3	2
Lack of Marketing Data	10	7	1
Lack of Marketing Support Services			
Product Adaptation		3	2
Integration of International Marketing	13	9	6
No Response		2	
Trade Barriers	7	2	3
Scarcity of Personnel	3		3

2. Domestic and International
   Marketing Differences

	Industry	Consumer	Other
Domestic Consumer Orientation		3	1
Greater International Regulation	13	6	9
Need for More Data -- International	6	1	3
Need for More Feedback/Control-- International	5	7	2
Less Awareness of International Problems by Top Management	6	7	1
Need To Integrate International Marketing at Corporate Level	4	2	1
at Division Level	6	4	
No Difference	6	5	4
Other/Multiple Unranked	2	4	6
No Response	2		

3. Personnel Selection Criteria

	Industry	Consumer	Other
Foreign National Status	9	7	13
Expressed Interest	6	9	3
Prior Formal Training	3	7	2
Foreign Language Ability	1		1
Domestic Marketing Ability	25	14	7
Preparation for Greater Domestic Responsibility	3	2	1
No Response	3		

4. Method of Conducting Program

	Primary Customer		
	Industry	*Consumer*	*Other*
Domestic on-the-job Training	20	19	11
International on-the-job Training	18	12	7
Formal Corporate Program	4	4	3
Formal Outside Program	1		
Seminar Type Courses		1	
Other/Multiple Unranked	4	2	6
No Response	3	1	

5. Who Conducts Program

	Industry	*Consumer*	*Other*
Marketing Department	7	6	4
International Division	14	16	9
International Marketing Group	15	8	3
Functional Supervisor	5	6	5
Professional Association		1	
College/University			
Other/Multiple Unranked	4	2	3
No Response	5		3

6. Levels at Which Program is Offered

	Industry	*Consumer*	*Other*
Corporate	1	1	2
Division	20	7	8
Regional	4	4	
Individual Country		5	2
All Levels	6	7	6
No Internal Programs	5	3	6
No Response	3	3	2
Where needed or No Particular Level	8	8	4

7. Program Primary Objective

	Industry	*Consumer*	*Other*
Overall Survey	12	13	5
Stress Concrete Characteristics	3	4	3
Demonstrate Abstract Differences	1	2	1
Integration of International Marketing Within Firm	18	5	4
Other/Multiple Unranked	8	10	10
No Response	8	5	4

8. Expected Changes in Program	Primary Customer		
	Industry	*Consumer*	*Other*
Increased Emphasis on Product Adaptability	8	6	1
Increased Emphasis on Sales and Distribution Techniques	7	11	11
Increased Emphasis on Local Variations, e.g., Language	2	2	
Increased Emphasis on Socio-Political Aspects	1	1	2
Increased Emphasis on Integrating International Marketing	23	14	2
No Response	5	3	5
Structural Changes, Such as Introduction of Formal Training Programs	1	2	9

9. Reason for Change			
Introduction of More Sophisticated Products	7	7	5
Greater Consumer Orientation	1	12	2
Greater Cooperation With Local Interests	3	5	1
More Effective Local Competition	8	5	6
Development of Overall International Market	19	7	8
Other/Multiple Unranked	4	3	6
No Response	5	1	1

10. Foreign Environment Training			
Specifics Such as Language	10	6	2
Concepts Such as Socio-Cultural Differences	5	1	
Marketing Techniques Peculiar to Overseas Operations	27	15	27
Other/Multiple Unranked	3	2	4
No Response	6	4	5

11. Expected Changes			
Greater Stress on Empathy	1	9	2
Greater Stress on Product Knowledge	7	9	5
Greater Stress on Consumer Identification	6	4	2
Trend to World Customer	16	2	1
No Change	9	10	7
Other/Multiple Unranked	2	1	3
No Response	9	4	7

12. Transferability of
    Marketing Skills

	Primary Customer		
	Industry	*Consumer*	*Other*
Domestic Transferable to International	13	8	5
International Transferable to Domestic	3	1	
Neither Transferable	1		2
Mutually Transferable	20	13	7
Depends on Individual	13	16	10
Other/Multiple Unranked		1	3

13. Difficulties Facing Interna-
    tional Marketing Personnel

Different Standard of Living	4	8	8
Language Barrier	4	1	5
Different Cultural Concepts	19	10	10
Being Out of Corporate Mainstream	20	13	4
Other/Multiple Unranked		1	4
No Response	2	1	2

14. Characteristics Favoring Success

Foreign Language Ability	2	2	
Empathy With Foreign Environment	11	11	
Domestic Marketing Experience	16	7	3
Desire to Work Overseas	9	3	2
College/University Training	1	1	2
Corporate International Marketing Training	3	2	2
Being National of Country to Which Assigned	6	6	6
Other/Multiple Unranked	2	6	5
No Response		1	1

15. Supply of Qualified
    Personnel Today

Greater Than Demand	7	5	2
Less Than Demand	30	24	19
Equal to Demand	12	8	5
No Response	1	2	1

16. Supply of Qualified Personnel Within Five Years

	Primary Customer		
	Industry	*Consumer*	*Other*
Greater Than Demand	5	4	1
Less Than Demand	31	24	13
Equal to Demand	14	8	12
No Response		3	1

17. Cause of Shortage Today

	Industry	Consumer	Other
Unwillingness to Live Abroad	9	9	2
Lack of College Level Programs	2	2	1
Abstract Nature of International Marketing	9	7	2
No Shortage	11	5	6
Other/Multiple Unranked	12	14	13
No Response	7	2	3

18. Cause of Shortage Within Five Years

	Industry	Consumer	Other
Unwillingness to Live Abroad	12	8	2
Lack of College Level Programs	1		
Abstract Nature of International Marketing	8	7	
No Shortage	9	4	8
Other/Multiple Unranked	11	9	8
No Response	9	11	9

N O T E S

[Footnote references are given in full in the bibliography.]

INTRODUCTION

1. This point is discussed in most of the recent literature on international business. For a full treatment, see John Fayerweather *et. al., International Business Education: Curriculum Planning.* See also Lee C. Nehrt *et. al., International Business Research: Past, Present and Future.*

2. For additional comments, see A. Kapoor, "Educating the Visiting V.I.P. on Local Problems Abroad."

3. For further elaboration, see James A. Lee, "Cultural Analysis in Overseas Operations."

4. See A. Kapoor, "Business-Government Relations Become Respectable." See also Yair Aharoni, *The Foreign Investment Decision Process,* p. 94.

5. Dimitrios N. Chorafas, *Developing the International Executive,* p. 12.

6. For additional comments see prepared statement by Judd Polk, "The Internationalization of Production." Prepared for Hearings before the Subcommittee and Foreign Economic Policy of the Joint Economic Committee, Congress of the United States, Ninety-first Congress, Second Session, pp. 772-779.

7. Michael G. Duerr and James Greene, *The Problems Facing International Management: A Survey,* pp. 2 and 11.

8. Richard F. Gonzales and Anant R. Negandhi, *The United States Overseas Executive: His Orientation and Career Patterns,* p. 4. See also Francis X. Hodgson, "The Selection of Overseas Management" in *World Marketing: A Multinational Approach,* edited by John Ryans, Jr. and James C. Baker.

9. Enid Baird Lovell, *The Changing Role of the International Executive*, p. 5.

10. Gonzales and Negandhi, p. 5.

11. See John M. Ivancevich, "Selection of American Managers for Overseas Assignments" (Unpublished). See also John M. Ivancevich and James C. Baker, "Job Satisfaction of American Managers Overseas." *MSU Business Topics*, Summer, 1969.

12. Lovell, p. 1.

13. Chorafas, p. 12.

CHAPTER 3

1. For a detailed discussion, see Jack N. Behrman, *Some Patterns in the Rise of the Multinational Enterprise.*

2. See R. J. Alymer, "Who makes Marketing Decisions in the Multinational Firm?" and Warren J. Keegan, "Multinational Marketing: The Headquarters Roll."

3. See Warren J. Keegan, "Multinational Product Planning," Montrose Sommers and Jerome Kerman, "Why Products Flourish Here, Fizzle There," and Robert D. Buzzell, "Can you Standardize Multinational Marketing?"

4. An example of a trend in this direction is the interest of Ford Motor Company to develop an automobile which is specifically designed for the needs of Southeast Asian countries. See *Time*, March 8, 1971, p. 79.

5. See William M. Reddig, "The New Multinational Manager," pp. 35-41.

6. For additional comments, see Michael Yoshino, "Marketing Orientation in International Business."

SELECTED BIBLIOGRAPHY

Books and Articles

Aharoni, Yair. *The Foreign Investment Decision Process.*
Boston: Division of Research, Graduate School of
Business Administration, Harvard University, 1966.

Alsegg, Robert, J. *Researching the European Markets.*
New York: American Management Association Research
Study No. 95, 1969.

Alymer, R. J. "Who makes Marketing Decisions in the Multinational Firm?" *Journal of Marketing,* October,
1970.

Behrman, Jack N. *Some Patterns in the Rise of the Multi-
national Enterprise.* Research Paper No. 18. Chapel
Hill, North Carolina: Graduate School of Business
Administration, 1969.

Boddewyn, J. *Comparative Management and Marketing: Text
and Readings.* Glenview, Illinois: Scott Foresman and
Co., 1969.

Buzzell, Robert D. "Can You Standardize Multinational
Marketing?" *Harvard Business Review,* November-
December 1968.

Carson, David. *International Marketing: A Comparative
Systems Approach.* New York: John Wiley and Sons,
Inc., 1967.

Chorafas, Dimitrios N. *Developing the International
Executive.* New York: American Management Association, Inc., 1967.

Directory of American Firms Operating in Foreign Countries.
New York: Simon & Schuster, Inc., 1969.

Duerr, Michael G., and James Greene. *The Problems Facing
International Management: A Survey.* New York:
National Industrial Conference Board, Inc., 1968.

87

Fayerweather, John, *et al.* *International Business Education: Curriculum Planning*. New York: Graduate School of Business Administration, New York University, 1966.

Gonzales, Richard F., and Anant R. Negandhi. *The United States Overseas Executive: His Orientation and Career Patterns*. East Lansing, Michigan: Michigan State University, 1967.

Ivancevich, John M. "Selection of American Managers for Overseas Assignments." Unpublished.

———, and James C. Baker. "Job Satisfaction of American Managers Overseas." *MSU Business Topics,* Summer, 1969.

Kapoor, A. *International Business Negotiations: A Study in India*. New York: New York University Press, 1970.

———. "Business-Government Relations Become Respectable." *Columbia Journal of World Business,* July-August, 1970.

———. "Educating the Visiting V.I.P. on Local Problems Abroad." *Worldwide P & I Planning,* November-December, 1970.

———, and Phillip D. Grub, eds. *The Multinational Enterprise in Transition*. Princeton, New Jersey: The Darwin Press, Inc., forthcoming.

Keegan, Warren J. "Multinational Product Planning." *Journal of Marketing,* January, 1969.

———. "Multinational Marketing: The Headquarters Role." *Columbia Journal of World Business,* January-February, 1971.

Lee, James A. "Cultural Analysis in Overseas Operations." *Harvard Business Review,* March-April, 1966.

Lovell, Enid Baird. *The Changing Role of the International Executive*. New York: National Industrial Conference Board, Inc., 1966.

Montana, Patrick J. *The Marketing Executive of the Future*. Binghampton, New York: Vail-Ballou Press, Inc., 1967.

Moody's Industrial Manual. New York: Moody's Investors Service, Inc., 1969.

Nehrt, Lee C., *et al. International Business Research: Past, Present, and Future*. Bloomington, Indiana: Bureau of Business Research, Graduate School of Business, Indiana University, 1970.

Poor's Register of Corporations, Directors, and Executives. New York: Standard & Poor's Corporation, 1970.

Reddig, William M. "The New Multinational Manager." *Saturday Review,* November 22, 1969.

Robinson, Richard R. *International Business Policy.* New York: Holt, Rinehart and Winston, Inc., 1965.

Ryans, John K. "Is it too soon to Put a Tiger in Every Tank?" *Columbia Journal of World Business,* March-April 1969.

————, and James C. Baker, eds. *World Marketing: A Multinational Approach.* New York: John Wiley and Sons, Inc., 1967.

Sommers, Montrose, and Jerome Kerman. "Why Products Flourish Here, Fizzle There." *Columbia Journal of World Business,* Marcn-April, 1967.

Yoshino, Michael Y. "Marketing Orientation in International Business." *Business Topics 13* (Summer, 1965).